Take my Hand

Written by Kathy Meenach

This book was created to spark joyful memories for seniors.

As a caregiver, whether you are a family member, friend, hired helper or volunteer, take a moment to read with a senior to experience these memories together.

May you both have moments of happiness and make new memories to cherish.

Love, *Kathy*

To families that create and hold loving memories in their hearts, to pass on for generations to come.

Spring

Take my hand, as we walk down the
sidewalk lined with trees dressed in bright
spring-green leaves alongside dogwood
trees with white and pink blooms.

Is that a bird's nest I see nestled in the branches of a spruce tree? Watch, as the Robins add twigs and moss to the nest. Soon, Mother Robin will lay eggs of sky blue and sit on the nest until her babies have hatched.

Look at all the spring blooms in this yard. Daffodils
and tulips, amongst the azaleas, nod in the breeze.
The branches of yellow forsythia flowers reach towards
the purple clusters of wisteria covering the arbor nearby.
Neighbors wave from their big, sunny porch as we pass by.

Here comes a friend walking their dog.
They stop to say hello and share a smile.
With a "woof" and a wagging tail, the dog
sits for a pat on the head. We laugh and
continue to enjoy this beautiful day.

Summer

Take my hand as we walk along the shore, the waves lapping
at our feet and our toes digging into the sand. Smell the salty air.

Seagulls and pelicans fly overhead in the clear, blue sky. A breeze blows through our hair, carrying the sounds of the seagulls calling in the air.

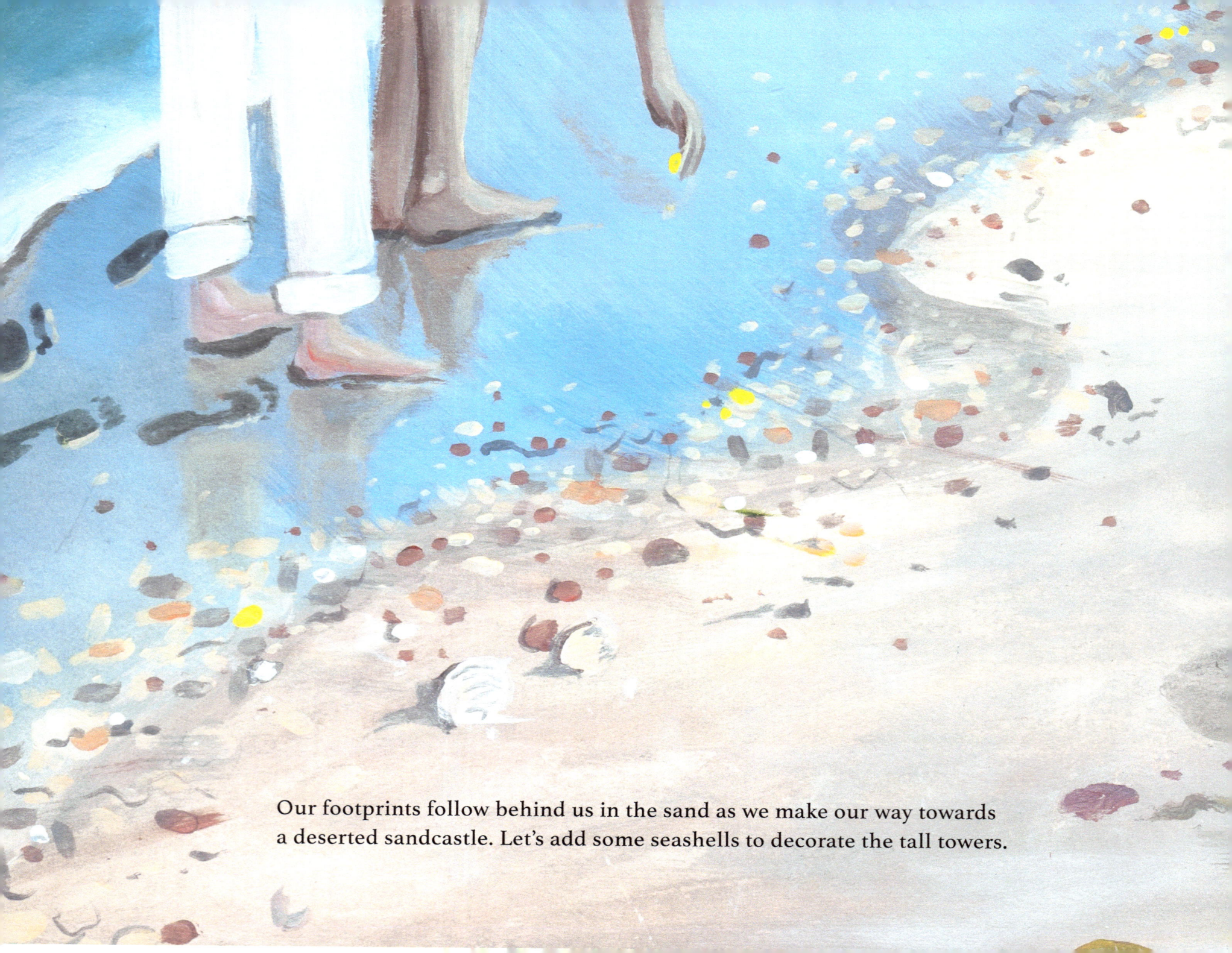

Our footprints follow behind us in the sand as we make our way towards a deserted sandcastle. Let's add some seashells to decorate the tall towers.

What treasures can we find on the shore? A sand dollar or feather, the bright gleam of a piece of sea glass, skittering sand crabs or a conch shell. Now hold it up to your ear... can you hear the ocean?

Fall

Take my hand as we ride through curving roads in the mountains.
Look out the windows at the trees filled with Autumn leaves
turning yellow, orange, red, and golden brown.

Let's stop at this apple orchard stand. Breathe in the crispness of the air with the sweet smell of ripe apples. Which will we choose? McIntosh, Granny Smith, Winesap or Golden Delicious. Some hot apple cider with cinnamon tastes cozy.

We walk through a Fall Festival passing booths of 1st place winners for biggest pig, best hand sewn quilt, jars of canned vegetables, fruit, jellies and jams and a child's drawing of a funny scarecrow. To our delight, vendors offer corn dogs, funnel cakes, cotton candy and bright red candy apples.

PUMPKIN PATCH

As we wind back down the mountain, we spy a pumpkin patch. Tall bundles of dried cornhusk stalks adorn the entrance. The sound of laughing children makes us smile as they join their parents in picking out the best pumpkin. We'll find a special one to carve into a Jack 'O Lantern and sit it on the front porch, glowing for Halloween.

Winter

Take my hand as we walk in the quiet of the winter woods. We wear our sweaters and heavy coats with warm woolen scarves, hats and gloves. See your breath in the air as we step onto the path.

Our boots crunch in the snow. The trees are covered in white. A cardinal flies by, landing on a branch with hanging icicles. His brilliant red feathers flutter in the shining sunlight.

Maybe we'll see a deer with big antlers or footprints in the snow of a raccoon or fox. A rabbit hops out on the trail with long ears and nose twitching, watchful for any sudden movement. Listen...can you hear the crows cawing to one another?

Softly, snow begins to fall. If we look quickly, we can see all the beautiful shapes of snowflakes falling on our jacket sleeves. As we turn to go back home, we look with wonder and feel the peaceful solitude that nature brings.

ACKNOWLEDGEMENTS

My beautiful Momma is the inspiration for this book. Her stories and loving tradition of family are heartfelt and bring her great joy. Seeing her blue eyes light up with a smile or laugh as she recounts a favorite moment in her life, is what love is all about. I am blessed to have her in my life.

Thank you to my publisher at Fernhead Publishing, Lisa Andrews, for her unwavering support and encouragement of my stories, vision and written word.

Thank you to my illustrator, Olivia Baker, for beautifully bringing my written words to life.

Thank you to my daughter, Tasha Lund, for her incredible talent as a digital designer who formatted this book with collaborative vision.

Thank you to all my family, friends and people in my life that have lovingly supported my dreams and visions. It is through you, my creativity blossoms.

NON-PROFIT ORGANIZATIONS

♥

Listed below are some wonderful organizations that assist through
programs and research to help people with memory loss related diseases.

ALZHEIMER'S FOUNDATION OF AMERICA

The mission of the Alzheimer's Foundation of America (AFA) is to provide
support, services and education to individuals, families and caregivers
affected by Alzheimer's disease and related dementias nationwide, and
fund research for better treatment and a cure.

Website: alzfdn.org   **Email:** info@alzfdn.org   **Phone:** 866-232-8484

DEMENTIA SPRING FOUNDATION

The Dementia Spring Foundation is a bridge between the dementia and arts communities.
Dementia Spring supports artists and arts organizations producing original visual artwork
depicting dementia and initiating programs infusing creativity in dementia care, respectively.
Harnessing creativity to foster community and hope, Dementia Spring seeks to inspire joy
among those living with dementia and Alzheimer's disease and their families.

Website: dementiaspring.org   **Email:** info@dementiaspring.org

BRIGHTFOCUS FOUNDATION

BrightFocus funds exceptional scientific research worldwide to defeat
Alzheimer's disease, macular degeneration, and glaucoma and provides
expert information on these heartbreaking diseases.

Website: brightfocus.org   **Email:** info@brightfocus.org   **Phone:** 800-437-2423

DEMENTIA SOCIETY OF AMERICA

Our programs bring much-needed education, local resources, and life
enrichment to individuals and families impacted by Dementia. To enhance the
quality of life for those living with Dementia, caregivers, and the community!

Website: dementiasociety.org   **Email:** info@dementiaiasociety.org   **Phone:** 800-336-3684

ABOUT THE ILLUSTRATOR

Olivia Baker, a Virginia based artist, holds degrees from the University of Virginia in evolutionary biology and studio art. Her murals and paintings explore themes relating to ecology and the Anthropocene.

More work can be viewed livibakerart.com

ABOUT THE AUTHOR

Kathy Meenach's writing captures her joy for life and meaningful memories created with family, friends and people. Through her descriptive words she draws the reader in, to experience shared moments of everyday life. Inspired by her parents, Kathy has written "Take My Hand" as a gift to treasure with seniors or those with memory loss. She has also written "Sojourns, A Guide to Rejuvenation" inspired by her travels, gaining a spiritual connection to different landscapes, people and traditions.

Where to find Kathy's books

Fernhead Publishing: fernheadpublishing.com/kathy-meenach

Amazon: amazon.com (hardback, eBook)

Contact Kathy to purchase directly

Where to find Kathy

Instagram: @sojournswithkathy

Email: kathy@fernheadpublishing.com

www.ingramcontent.com/pod-product-compliance
Lightning Source LLC
Chambersburg PA
CBHW041653260326

41914CB00018B/1631